DOROTHY THOMPSON'S
Political Guide

DOROTHY THOMPSON'S
Political Guide

A STUDY OF AMERICAN LIBERALISM

AND ITS RELATIONSHIP TO MODERN

TOTALITARIAN STATES

STACKPOLE SONS • PUBLISHERS
NEW YORK

For the privilege of using material in this book
the publishers are grateful to the editors of GOOD
HOUSEKEEPING and THE LADIES' HOME JOURNAL

*Manufactured entirely by The Telegraph Press
in Harrisburg, Pennsylvania*

CONTENTS

DOROTHY THOMPSON'S
Political Guide

I

FIFTY million isms must be wrong. On the face of it, some of them *must* be! Capitalism, Socialism, Communism, Naziism, Fascism, Collectivism, Nationalism, Internationalism, Totalitarianism—the words are not all in the dictionary, but they are in every newspaper that we pick up. Ideologies! Words! Faiths! Creeds!

For the sake of these words and what they represent, men wear black shirts or brown, put red ties around their necks, conspire in cafés and drawing rooms, quarrel with their friends, desert their parents, parade, shout, make camps, publish newspapers, proclaim that a new heaven and a new earth are at hand.

For the sake of these words, and what they represent, bombs fall: yesterday in Ethiopia, today in China and in Spain, tomorrow—where? Nobody knows, and so eleven percent of the total production of wealth in the world is spent for armaments.

11

Across Europe the air is thick with contending isms. Italy broadcasts in English to England and in Arabic to England's colonies. England, at long last, replies—in seven languages. Russia erects radio stations of especially powerful wave lengths, hoping to crash into some German sitting room with its ism. Germany makes it a penal offense to turn on the radio to Russia or Switzerland, and broadcasts in English to England and America, in French to Paris, in Spanish to South America.

Because of isms at least four million people are homeless. The man without a country is the twentieth-century phenomenon! Russian aristocrats and Polish and German and Austrian Jews; German socialists and Russian capitalists; Italian democrats and Italian anarchists. Politicians and artists, professors and beggars. Rich men and poor men. Austrian free-thinkers and Spanish Catholics. They carry League of Nations passports, or fake passports, or passports good for any country other than their own. They beat on a thousand doors, they crave admittance, they marry to get one citizenship or divorce to get another.

Because of isms flags that have flown for generations are pulled down. New ones go up.

Thrones totter, parliaments dissolve, leaders emerge. Songs and slogans: Arise, ye prisoners of starvation! *Giovanezza! Heil* Hitler! Stalin is our Leader!

Oh, say can you see? Oh, say, does the Star-Spangled Banner yet wave? Yes, but it's getting increasingly hard to see. It is lost in a fog of isms. This book is intended to be a political dictionary —the intelligent Woman's Guide to Isms.

What is an ideology?

A system of ideas. Or what passes for a system of ideas. In the sense in which it is continually used in the daily press, an ideology is a creed to which groups of people—sometimes a minority, sometimes a majority, sometimes (by edict) everybody in a given nation—subscribe or are supposed to subscribe.

Fascism, Communism, Democracy, are all "ideologies." We are confining ourselves to current political and economic ideologies.

What is Collectivism?

Whether it is the major superstition or the major illusion or the great solution of the twentieth century is a matter of opinion. I leave that to you. Collectivism is any form of social, economic, and political organization in which all production, distribution, and a more or less large part of the individual's whole life are strictly subjected to the aim and purpose of the whole society.

In a collectivist society man is not considered as a being endowed with "certain inalienable rights," such as those enumerated in the Bill of Rights and other articles of the American Constitution, which include the right to worship as he pleases, to work where and at what he likes, to make individual contracts, to speak his mind, and to keep and spend or invest what he earns; in a collectivist state all these rights are subject to the prevailing interpretation of social objectives.

Fascism, Naziism, and Communism are all Collectivisms. In this respect they are all alike.

What is Totalitarianism?

The word was invented within the last fifteen years, to describe a form of state that actually exists. That is the state which regulates everything. It was described by Mussolini, "Every-

thing for the state; nothing apart from the state."
In the totalitarian state, government lays a claim
upon every phase of life. It may exempt certain
activities. Mussolini, for instance, allows his
people some religious freedom. So does Hitler,
but it is much restricted, and many religious organizations have been dissolved, and others are
being consciously undermined. But these exemp-
tions are only favors; they are not rights. The
state has the right to take them away tomorrow.
The state alone has any "rights."

In the totalitarian state, every single human
activity: religion, education, work, business,
even the relations between individuals—love,
marriage—are all geared into line with a single
central policy. All private organizations,
whether they are philanthropic, social, or economic—women's clubs, academies of science or
art, or employers' organizations or trade unions
— must also be geared into line with the state's
program. The Rotary Club is banished in Germany because it is international. So are the
Masonic orders.

Russia, Italy, and Germany are all totalitarian
states.

What is Communism?

Communism is a very old faith, held for centuries, from time to time, by groups of people. Originally it meant any form of social organization in which all production was for common and equal distribution. But in our modern political dictionary it means that philosophy of history, that form of organization, and strategy held by Karl Marx, who wrote in the middle of the last century and is the founder of modern Communism. It is supposed to have been put into practice in Soviet Russia, and the Communist International, the so-called Comintern, which exists to further this gospel throughout the world, is dominated by the political leaders of Soviet Russia, who lay down the "party line" or party policy which all communists throughout the world are supposed to follow with strict discipline. Members who fail to do so are "purged" out of the party ranks, whether they are citizens of Paris or London or New York.

The basic idea of modern Communism is the class struggle. Communists believe that all existing forms of government, except that of the Soviets, are merely instruments of the owning classes. It is the business of the working classes, or all the people who own no property, to organize and make a new state. Until 1933, the Communist International held the belief that there was no way of overthrowing these other forms of government except by armed uprising and revolution, and they considered all socialists and reformers who tried to change the state by non-revolutionary methods as the worst enemies of the working classes.

But when Fascism triumphed in Germany and openly announced itself as the world enemy of Communism, the Communist International feared that the Soviet State would be isolated and attacked by Germany, or possibly by Germany, Italy, and Japan, all together. Therefore the Communist International changed its policy, and instructed communists all over the world to cooperate with all left-wing or reform governments everywhere. The communist theory is that a world war is inevitable; that in that war, if they play their cards well, the democracies will be lined up against the fascist dictatorships, and that the result of the war will be the triumph of Communism all over the world. Their chief program now is to get the democracies so lined up.

The basic theory of Communism is: first, the

class struggle; and second, the dictatorship of the proletariat. This means, in practice, the dictatorship of the Communist Party. All industry, banking, and commerce is nationalized and run by the Party through the government, which it controls. No private property is tolerated except personal effects and such money as is invested in government savings banks or government loans. Nobody may employ any other person for wages, except by permission of the state, for such things as domestic service. Industry is run as a series of state trusts, and, with a tiny number of exceptions, everybody is in the employ of the state.

Now, ask me whether the products thus produced are equally distributed—for that was an original communist idea.

The answer is, they are *not!* Heads of state trusts, managers, and specially skilled workers get high wages; common labor gets low wages. Piecework has been reintroduced into factories, and a special speed-up process invented, called *Stakhanovism* (there's another ism). If the workers don't like it, they can lump it. Strikes are forbidden. People can vote—but only on the communist ticket. Inefficient work is called "sabotage" or "wrecking," and the perpetrators are shipped off to prison camps or perilous state projects in Siberia or Archangel. "Enemies of the state"—and the state decides who is an enemy—are forbidden work cards, and not counted as unemployed. They can starve. Military service is universal and compulsory.

In practice Communism is the organization of a nation into one big corporation of interlocking trusts, with the control vested in the hands of self-appointed politicians, under a dictator, and they can determine wages and hours of labor, and distribute or invest the profits as they see fit. Some proportion of the profits—no one knows exactly how much—is used to spread propaganda in other countries.

What is Fascism?

Fascism is another kind of Collectivism. Both Fascism and Naziism are the total organization of all the people in the state, under the banner of nationalism. The working class is the idol of Communism. The nation is the idol of Fascism and Naziism. Complete sacrifice of the individual is demanded by Communism for the sake of the world revolution. It is demanded by Fascism or Naziism for the sake of Italy or Germany.

19

Fascism has always presented itself as the protector of private property against Communism. It was invented, however, by a socialist: Benito Mussolini. In the fascist states private enterprise is permitted, but it is so rigidly controlled that the owner really becomes a trustee of the state, which can and does determine whether he may purchase raw materials, how he shall invest his money, what his profits may or may not be, and what the conditions of labor may be in his factories. The needs of the state determine what is produced, how it is produced, and how it is distributed.

In fascist countries, just as in Soviet Russia, only one political party is permitted, and this party is not democratically formed but is "authoritarian" (there's another ism: Authoritarianism), which means that it is organized like an army, from the top down. Not every citizen can join it. In Germany the ranks of the Nazi Party were closed in 1933. It is harder to get into the Communist Party in Russia than into an exclusive New York club. You are taken on probation, and kept or thrown out, according to how you behave yourself.

Under Fascism (as under Communism) the party controls the policy and the machinery of the state; the state absorbs the work and life of the whole nation, and party-state-nation are one.

Naziism differs from Fascism very little in the actual form of organization. Both kinds of state are run by dictators and party-dominated bureaucracies. Naziism is unique, however, in that it has a racial philosophy. It maintains that the world is divided into Aryans and non-Aryans; that of all Aryans, Nordics are superior in mind, courage, and physique; and that the Teutons (Germans) are the highest representatives of the Nordic race and spirit. "Race is everything," says Hitler. Therefore all non-Aryans (particularly Jews) are forbidden to intermarry with Germans, are denied any positions in the state; and a rigorous campaign of calumny is carried on against them. Schools are established to train the future "élite," a ruling class who, according to Hitler, will direct the German state for the next thousand years.

Only such candidates are admitted to this new ruling class as can prove themselves of "pure" German blood for generations. The Nazi philosophy holds that once Germany has made herself racially pure, she will be invulnerable, since cross-breeding between races degenerates the stock. Nazi racialism is considered to be a world philosophy, and Nazi agents preach it in many countries besides their own.

Every reputable anthropologist in the world thinks that the Nazi racial theory is "pure" nonsense.

Socialism differs from Communism in several ways. First of all, socialists reject the leadership of Moscow and refuse to follow the Russian party line. Many socialists believe that Russia is not a socialist state at all, but just another form of Fascism. There are many sorts and groups of socialists. They all subscribe to the theory that the means of production—raw materials, land, industries—should either be owned by the community as a whole, or be administered, and their fruits distributed, in the interests of all. Socialism aims at the collective organization of the community in the interest of the masses of the people, by common ownership and collective control.

Christian socialists stress the corporate nature of society and the need for social solidarity on a religious basis.

Guild socialists—there are many in England, for instance—believe in ownership and control by guilds of workers, municipalities, cooperatives, and quasi-public corporations, rather than by a central government.

Fabianism, the parent of British Socialism, seeks "evolutionary" Socialism—not through the class struggle, but by permeating existing parties with socialistic ideas, the object being to secure a larger and more balanced production of wealth and a more equitable distribution of it.

Socialistic ideas of one sort or another have permeated the thinking of all governments in the world today, and they are as old as Greece. If Socialism is to be regarded as the antithesis of Individualism then Plato was a socialist. If the essence of Socialism is to believe that the common good must take precedence over individual interests, then most intelligent people are socialistic in their thinking. Every society in the world today believes that too large inequalities in income—immense riches and destitution—are undesirable. Every society in the world today affirms in its laws and customs that every child must be given a basic education at the public expense, that owners of factories must conform to standards of working conditions and hygiene, that child labor must be prohibited, that workers must have the right to organize and through organization secure decent conditions of hours and employment.

Almost all western countries today believe that the worker—that is to say, the man whose labor is his chief or only property—must be insured, partly at the public expense, against unemployment, sickness, and old age. Many countries provide the less well-to-do parts of the population with houses or apartments that are either partly paid for out of the public course, or are run without profit, or have their profits strictly limited by law.

All western countries heavily tax high incomes and huge inheritances both to obtain revenue for social purposes and to prevent vast accumulations of wealth in the hands of a few people, to be passed down from generation to generation.

All western countries provide "free" hospitals, orphanages, and asylums for those who are unable to purchase such care for themselves; and they are paid for, of course, out of the national income.

All western countries, where things of universal use—such as utilities and railroads—are still in private hands, control, through government, the rates which are permitted to be charged. They also control to some extent the uses to which land may be put. Many countries prohibit the felling of forests, except where the owner posts a bond to replant them in a specified number of years. Laws are passed to prevent land being so used that it becomes eroded. Building and zoning laws in cities prevent the individual from doing anything he pleases.

All these laws restrict the rights of private ownership or distribute the fruits of production for social purposes, regardless of whether the recipient has earned these fruits in open competition. Nevertheless, in all western countries most of the actual wealth is owned by private individuals, the great bulk of income is distributed in the form of wages or salaries, and new wealth is produced by private enterprise.

What is Capitalism?

The production of wealth by private enterprise is called Capitalism. It is hard to call Capitalism one of the isms, because Capitalism is not a creed at all. Capitalism was not "invented" by any sociologist or philosopher. Capitalists never called themselves that. The word was invented by socialists to describe what they hated.

Capitalism is the use of wealth in private hands to create more wealth. It is the existing world-wide modern system of organizing production and trade by private enterprise, free to seek profit by employing human labor. Its defenders argue that never, since the beginning of history, has there been such a thing as perfect equality and harmony; that acquisition has always gone with strength and skill; that Egypt and Babylon, ancient Greece and Rome, and every known period of history had rich and poor, and that actually modern technology, plus liberal democracy, plus an increased social sense, plus Capitalism, have created the modern world, and that as far as the standard of living of the average man is concerned the modern world surpasses all previous epochs of history.

They point out that this modern world of incredible riches, is the result of extremely complex organizations of human intelligence and labor, of man's inventiveness allowed to function freely; that many great undertakings which have produced income for tens of thousands of people have sprung from a single brain, or from half a dozen brains; that freedom to experiment, invent, invest, and promote, in the hope of profit, has concentrated millions of minds and all sorts of specialized intelligences upon thousands of problems. They insist that private enterprise and initiative, willing to take risks in the hope of gain, allowed to function in freedom, have produced the greatest wealth ever known in the history of mankind. And that if you stop this process and turn everything over to government, the activity will slow down, inventiveness will cease, and we shall get not equalization of riches, but equalization of poverty.

They claim, further, that the workers have steadily shared a larger and larger portion of the increased income from this wealth; that they will continue to increase their share as the total income increases; that, allowed to function freely, they can produce enough to enlarge the free social services; that Capitalism is a natural order of things, based upon man's nature and upon biological inequalities; that, although there is much injustice in it, there has never been a perfect world; and that injustice can be lessened by increased social consciousness and intelligence.

Public ownership—say the apologists for Capitalism—does not mean that the people own the wealth. That is pure illusion. It means that the state owns the wealth. But the state is not the people; it is a political organization. It will be controlled by individuals, by politicians, and they will have no competition. Rather, they will be in possession of the means of coercion, and will operate the whole mechanism chiefly in the interest of perpetuating themselves. They point out that men still work for wages, and very bad wages, in Soviet Russia, and that merit and capacity become, under Socialism or Communism, subservient to political reliability.

Many people today, who call themselves liberals, are socialists or collectivists of one kind or another. Historically, however, Liberalism is closely associated with Capitalism. The modern liberal who is not a socialist believes that Capitalism must be somewhat curbed in the interest of the public welfare. Many conservatives think the same thing, but are more cautious. But the British conservatives are at about the same point where the British Labor Party was ten years ago.

Something else, in the experience of the last fifteen years—during which all the news isms have come into being and many new Utopias have been founded—has made a great many people who once were socialists stop and think. So far, private enterprise and political democracy have gone hand in hand. When one has perished or been rigidly controlled, the other has perished also. The only countries left in the western world, where science is free, where art is uncontrolled, where men can write, speak, and think as they please, where the individual enjoys security in his person, against arrest without warrant and trial by jury without indictment, are capitalist countries. They are also the only countries which are not overwhelmingly militaristic. They are the United States, Great Britain, Holland, the Scandinavian countries, France, Switzerland, and some of the other small states. In all these countries Capitalism has been forced by taxation to distribute a larger portion of its annual income in the form of free services to the underprivileged and to collective enterprises shared by all the people. But where private enterprise has been abolished or placed under complete state control, civil liberties have been abolished, too.

It became the fashion a few years ago to say that civil liberties meant nothing to the average man; that his freedom was just freedom to starve. But it also happens that the "free" countries are those in which the underprivileged are best fed.

A great many people say that there is a great

battle going on in the world: between Fascism and Communism. Fascism is represented as Capitalism in its ultimate and final form, when it controls the state wholly. Communism is represented as the final expression of democracy.

But this theory was invented by fascists and communists.

To a democrat, looking on, it seems like a sham battle. We see Russia developing into a strongly centralized, highly nationalistic, intensely militarized state, subjecting policy and public welfare to national and military aims; and we see Mussolini nationalizing more and more enterprises, restricting private initiative more and more, while the economic dictator of Germany becomes, not the capitalist representative, Dr. Schacht, but General Goering, who is a soldier and aviator and who believes that the chief business of Capitalism is to produce more cannons.

In Spain we see a popular republican movement checked by a fascist attack, and then we watch the Russian-trained communist strategists with the loyalist forces take over and organize the loyalist army and make it into their instrument. We begin to fear that victory for either side will mean ruthless military dictatorship.

More and more people think, therefore, that the real struggle between ideologies in the world is not between these two isms, but between freedom and slavery; between a civilian order of things and military dictatorship.

Democracy for most of us is not an ism. It is a way of life. It does not represent any rigid form of state or national organization. It is something constantly developing and unfolding, changing from day to day, making mistakes, advancing in this direction and retreating in that, but always animated by a few fundamental ideas: that men have a right to live their own lives, provided they don't tread too heavily on other people's toes; that the human being is capable of harmonizing many allegiances—he can be, for instance, a good American and a good Catholic or Baptist or Christian Scientist; that the state is not endowed with any divine rights, but is merely a useful instrument invented by men to serve them; that man's business on earth is to improve himself and respect his neighbor; that the Golden Rule is as good a guide for individual and social conduct as any theory ever invented; that the individual shall be judged, not by his race, background, or national origins, but

31

by his human qualities of heart and mind and skill; that laws which everyone must obey should not be arbitrarily made, but should be the result of debate, deliberation, consultation; that power should be divided, not concentrated; and that by common effort we should try for improvement, but not attempt perfection. For perfection is the attribute of God.

II

ALL my life I have been a pacifist. All my life I have hated war and loved peace. I have contributed to peace societies, written for peace, spoken for peace, paraded for peace. But today I seriously question whether our ways of seeking peace are not playing directly into the hands of those who love war and intend to pursue it. I see the nations of the world arming in ways that have never before been known in the modern world. I am not speaking of new forms of poison gas, heavier or swifter bombing planes, or parachutes to land brigades of soldiers. It is true that the techniques of war are constantly "improved" as the genius of an age of invention is put in the service of the war machine. But that is not what is most disturbing. What is revolutionary is that the minds of men, women and children are being deliberately trained, directed, distorted, by every conceivable instrument of education and propaganda, to make them toler-

33

ant of war, receptive of war, prepared for war, lovers of war. The greatest menace in the world today is not poison gas. There are gas masks against that. The menace is poisoned words, poisoned ideas.

A hundred and fifty million Russians have been told over and over again, by their teachers, by their leaders, by their schoolbooks, that an Armageddon is coming in which world capitalism will confront world communism and communism will emerge triumphant. Sixty-five million Germans are being told every day, in every way, that cannons are more precious than butter; that war is the natural and inevitable condition of mankind; that the Fighting Hero is the apotheosis of Man, and that the German People are destined to expand and to rule and to change the face and character of the earth. Forty million Italians are trained to despise peace and to glory in war. And all of young Japan is brought up in admiration of the warrior as the highest type of citizen.

I have seen a German youth camp, housing six thousand children around the age of ten, display in tree-high letters the words: "You were born to die for Germany!" I have seen babies of six and seven, black-shirted and belted, march in

Italy in military drill. I have seen children in Russian kindergartens taught how to adjust gas masks and the strategy of trench warfare.

Once, wherever one might go in the world, one found men and women who shared one's own dream of peace, and were ready to use their influence with their own governments to help find new means of arbitration, to further general disarmament, to seek international collaboration. Today, whole nations are hermetically sealed to all such ideas. Today in Germany the winner of the last Nobel peace prize is considered a traitor, and to attend any peace meeting would make one a candidate for a concentration camp. Today in Italy there is only one morality: the power and glory of Italy. Today in Russia all children are brought up to despise and hate "the class enemy."

Russia is vast, with almost limitless resources. The conquest of Nature, the building of industry, the raising of the fertility of the soil, are likely to engage her energies for generations to come. Not the absence of war spirit, but the thousand and one moral substitutes for war which now engross the Russian interest, postpone Russian dreams of conquest. Or so it seems.

But no such considerations curb the desire of other dictatorships to expand. Within the last years we have seen Japan invade China in violation of numerous treaties and agreements, Italy invade Ethiopia in a cynically open war of conquest, whole German and Italian armies land in Spain to aid a military attack on a legal, parliamentary government.

Where will all this end, and does it not demand a revaluation of what we mean by keeping the peace? Does anyone really think that there will ever be peace except inside the general acceptance of certain principles and codes of international behavior? "It takes two to reach an agreement," says Hamilton Fish Armstrong in his gallant little polemic against dictatorship, called *We or They*, "but it only takes one to make a war." That is a plain statement of fact. Are we, then, going to say to aggressive nations, "Go ahead and make war whenever you please. So long as you don't touch us, it's no concern of ours?"

Actually that is what we are saying, with our present neutrality policy. We are saying, "Break treaties, invade other nations, bomb cities, blockade ports, starve women and children, and we will take our ships off the seas and fold our hands. You can count on our doing nothing." We contribute to world anarchy by such words, and hope that we, alone, will be spared the final results of that anarchy! But Emerson said: "Nothing can bring you peace but the triumph of principle."

Not one of us would adopt such a policy in our personal lives. All of us in our personal values draw a line between attacker and attacked, between those who choose violence and those who choose law. If we failed to take such an attitude, we would soon live in a state of complete barbarism. None of us has ever been taught to obtain peace by yielding to blackmail. In a world where anarchy rules, no one is safe. To think so is to say aloud in a community where a kidnaper is loose:

"Snatch anybody else's baby. So long as you don't take mine, I am not interested."

The world today is divided into two groups of nations: those whose leaders teach them a belief in violence, aggrandizement, that the end justifies the means, that success validates any procedure; and those who all too weakly cling to a belief in law, in the sanctity of treaties, and in settling disputes by arbitration. To the latter group still belong the greatest, strongest, richest and most stable nations on earth: the United States, the British Empire, France and her colonies, Switzerland, Holland and the little states of Northern Europe.

Those who have resigned from the common dream, the common faith, the common intention of international behavior according to law, are strong only in will power and ruthlessness. Yet that will power and ruthlessness have driven the world upon the defensive. Isn't it time, perhaps, to take an offensive? Would it not be wiser, and more conducive to peace, to say, "We want no war, but we shall not be blackmailed nor condone violence in others. We shall draw as closely as possible to those who think our thoughts and speak the language of our minds and hearts. We are not disinterested in the fate of free government in the world. All friends of order, law and arbitration are our friends. We shall support them when and as we see fit. Do not count upon our neutrality?"

The expression of such an attitude of mind does not commit us to wage war anywhere. But it would enormously strengthen and hearten the moral forces on the side of peace. Or so, at least, it seems to me.

Perhaps it seems so to me because I know now

that there are things for which I am prepared to die. I am willing to die for political freedom, for the right to give my loyalty to ideals above a nation or above a class, for the right to teach my child what I think to be truth, for the right to explore such knowledge as my brains can penetrate, for the right to love where my mind and heart admire without reference to some dictator's code to tell me what the national canons on the matter are, for the right to work with others of like mind, for a society which seems to me becoming to the dignity of the human race.

I shall pick no fight, nor seek to impose by force these standards on others. But let it be clear. If the fight comes unsolicited, I am not willing to die meekly, to surrender without an effort. And that being so, am I still a pacifist?

III

WHAT does it mean to be an American? What, in our tradition, is still vital and valid? What in our past demands clear repudiation? What kind of world do we want to live in? What do we really believe?

And why do we need to raise these questions at all?

"To some generations much is given. Of others much is expected. This generation of Americans has a rendezvous with Destiny."

With these words, the President of the United States accepted, in June of last year, the nomination of his party for re-election. The words impressed me, and have haunted me. For they express what is the continual background of our consciousness: the realization that the values to which we have traditionally given allegiance, the forms of social life and economic organization, the relationships between the individual and the community, between men and women, between parents and children—all are challenged. Many are in dissolution; some, apparently, are permanently destroyed. And we see all around us attempts to establish new values, new forms of social, political and economic organization. We see classes conflicting, and philosophies conflicting. And we face the future with uncertainty, if not with apprehension.

This decade, the decade of the 1930's, has been fateful for history. In it, the Soviet state, based upon a theory of history unique in application, and upon a conception of property at odds with what prevails elsewhere, has solidified itself for the first time in a written constitution. The Soviet state commands the territory of a sixth of the earth, and its size, natural wealth, and the vigor of its rapidly increasing population, all mean that what is happening there is bound vastly to influence the whole world for a long time to come. That influence may be positive or negative, but it is inescapable.

In Germany, an awakened national will, fed ever since the war on a sense of humiliation and injustice, broke out in this decade in a revolution which has not only overthrown the parliamentary state but has established the nation on a conception of racial solidarity and totalitarianism in the racial idea, which extends into every phase of life and thought, and affects even the teaching of science and art. In its political and economic organization, Germany has closely followed Italy, which made the change in the twenties.

Both Russian Communism and international Fascism are messianic and imperial. By that I mean that they seek to propagate their ideas abroad, either by grandiose propaganda or by direct interference in behalf of similarly minded groups in countries other than their own, or, in the case of the Fascist states, by military action. These attempts to influence the course of affairs all over the world are conscious, but the influence would exist in any case. Ideas travel, and cannot be isolated. The attempts of some of our school authorities to prevent students from learning anything about Communism, for instance, are futile. Newspapers exist; correspondents report; people travel. It is quite imposible to act as though Russia did not exist, or were as inaccessible and mysterious as Mars.

But the real reason why these experiments abroad influence our thought and produce unrest is that, for better or for worse, they are affirmative. The people, or at least those who speak for them, in Russia, Germany and Italy know very definitely what they believe, and what they intend to do. They are therefore nations which are going somewhere. And the consciousness of going somewhere is almost a definition of a nation. An agglomeration of people, held together merely by convenience, or apathy, or geography, is hardly a nation at all. It is possible that these nations which, through revolution, have established new foundations of action and belief under a new form of collective life are going to war or to their own destruction. Or it is possible that Russia will survive and the other systems not, or vice versa. But, for the moment, they represent in the world aggressive affirmation of something.

And the reason why the democratic nations are so weak in resistance—and they are weak— is that the democratic nations do not know with even a degree of definiteness what they believe, and what they want to do. Their political and economic behavior is habit, and hardly more. Their attitudes and actions have no clear philosophical foundation. We still speak of "Liberty" and "Democracy," but every second American, like every second Englishman and Frenchman, if he thinks at all, has a different idea of what "liberty" and "democracy" mean. Mr. John L. Lewis, for instance, thinks they mean something different from what Mr. Henry Ford thinks they mean. Most of our industrial workers are beginning to follow tendencies profoundly different from the prevailing ideas of our farmers. Can a society continue to exist without a deeply held common faith, or without a purpose? History would seem to indicate that it cannot.

A great many people thought that when President Roosevelt was elected in 1933 we, too, had made a revolution of sorts, and that the New Deal meant a fundamental change in American life. But when we look thoughtfully at what we have done, it is impossible to believe that anything of the kind has happened. The process of disintegrating confidence in what existed before has gone a long way farther, under the many experiments we have undertaken, but nothing has emerged to reintegrate the public faith. There is hardly an institution of our life in which the ordinary man retains undiminished belief. He doubts the integrity of our banking system; he doubts the industrialists, whom he has been taught to regard as "economic royalists"; he has seen his supreme legislative bodies, the two houses of Congress, capitulate in a manner unique in their history and develop no distinguished leadership. He is divided in his feelings about the Supreme Court. If he is a workingman, he has to choose between two labor leaderships at open war with each other, neither of which presents a sensible program.

Even the ignorant man, not accustomed to formulating his thoughts precisely or articulately, senses and feels that an epoch in American life is over. He no longer has faith in the shibboleths which dominated our country in the long period from the Civil War, through the Great War, to the Depression. The talk of rugged individualism leaves him cold, because he has experienced, in his own life, that economic catastrophes can occur to him which he is powerless to avert or overcome, no matter how thrifty or how proudly independent he may have thought himself. He knows that very few men can insure themselves by their own efforts against hazards which are due to unbalances in our collective and corporate life. He senses, however vaguely, that there has been something "rotten in Denmark" for a long time. Indeed, his intuitions in this respect are often much sounder than those of people who, by exceptional good fortune or superior energies, have managed to escape the worst effects of these chaotic years.

The ordinary man, the common man, is discontented with his society, and this discontent he shares with all people of sensitivity. Our writers and poets, in so far as they are gifted with sensibility, display distaste and revulsion.

These facts and these feelings lay behind the popular revolt in 1933 which gave us the New Deal. But today, five years later, a disillusionment is growing which, however, is nihilistic, because it does not know what it wants instead. A realization is dawning that nothing fundamental is being done to revive the promise of American life. The New Deal has enormously increased the sense of awareness; it has contributed radically to the breakdown of confidence in the forms and procedures of yesterday. But it has offered us no comprehensible picture of a future in which we can believe. We cannot believe that this vague eleemosynary humanitarianism, coupled with ruthless aggrandizement by politicians, is a picture of a new heaven and a new earth. We have not had a revival or a conversion—to use evangelical terms—we have just had a Christmas party for the other side of the railroad tracks, with a general distribution of governmental largess and a redistribution of privileges. We have laid no firm foundations under social justice. We have merely changed the composition of predatory groups.

Or so, at least, it seems to me. And it seems to me that if democracy is to become again a proud word, then this nation must redefine its whole attitude toward the things it is supposed to live by.

Can it be done? Not by any one of us, but, perhaps, by many of us, all attempting to do the same thing.

IV

IS NOT, perhaps, the education of our youth too mechanical and utilitarian? Our children, it seems to me, learn the history of events, but are woefully unversed in the history of thought. We teach "economics"; which is a bastard word, for there is no such thing as "economics," but only "political economy," the forms and uses of wealth in relation to specific ways of communal life. In our colleges, philosophy has yielded nearly everywhere to "psychology." Many of our history professors now teach our youth to interpret history from the standpoint of the characters or material condition of the men who set events in motion; thus, the Constitution of the United States is read by some wholly in the light of the economic status of the men who framed it, the presumption being that if they were well-to-do, they were incapable of disinterested thinking, and only concerned with a form of government in their own interest.

The result of this kind of teaching is to diminish all respect for intellect, reason and experience. Yet intellect, reason and experience furnish the only guides which mankind has ever had in its course, individually or collectively, through this world. Without recourse to them, we live without any standards, and to live without standards is a definition of barbarism. It is unavailing to point to our technical progress, our magnificent roads, our pleasant towns, our highly organized factories, as proof that we are civilized. These may be only the remnants of a civilization already in decay; they are not, of themselves, a guaranty against a new flood of barbarism.

When we read in the newspapers that a high official in German educational life asserts that the German people are no longer interested in truth, for the sake of truth, but acknowledge as truth only that which serves the interests of the Nazi state, we are hearing a barbarous statement. When we see governments offering no more reason for their actions than that a Hitler, a Stalin or a Mussolini demands them, or, as we now hear at home, that the majority has given a blanket mandate, we are also listening to barbarian voices. For the civilized man is bound to measure his beliefs and justify his actions by other standards than these. He must have some point of reference which he can hold to be intellectually valid, until reason and experience demonstrate a new truth or expand an old one.

These few words are only a preface to making this point: that the form of government which came into being on this continent at the end of the eighteenth century was the product of an age of reason, and was devised by one of the most extraordinary groups of men who ever gathered together in any country at any time. They were, in the most precise sense of the term, a group of aristocrats. By this I do not mean that they were rich and highly born, but that they were men of extraordinary abilities, who towered so high above the level of their times, and most times since, that they commanded the respect of the whole civilized world, and this despite the fact that they were citizens of a still uncouth and unformed country.

They were men of exceptional mental capacity and deep culture. In the papers existing from that time, they showed themselves to be familiar with the history, the constitutions and the political experiences of most preceding civilizations, and to have devoted the most exacting reasoning processes to the Constitution which they worked out and defended. Hamilton, Madison, Monroe, Franklin, Adams, John Jay were men who had applied their minds to the question of how republics were born; what threats existed internally and externally to destroy them; what conditions were favorable to their survival. To the consideration of these questions they brought learning, thought of remarkable disinterestedness, and the accumulated experience available to the students of that day.

Hamilton, Madison and John Jay defended the new Constitution in a series of eighty-five editorials addressed "To the People of the State of New York," and published in the newspapers of the time. Together they constitute the Federalist, probably the greatest treatise on government which had appeared in the world since Aristotle's Politics—with which, incidentally, the defenders of the Constitution showed themselves thoroughly familiar. It is perfectly amazing to me that an American boy or girl can graduate today from an American university without ever having had thoroughly to study and pass an examination on these American documents, which are on a plane of thought with Plato's Republic, Aristotle's Politics and Machiavelli's Prince. The mere fact that this is so is evidence of how little we care about thought and its history.

It is a commonplace now to talk about "horse and buggy days"; but 1787, when The Federalist was written, was much farther removed from the fourth century B. C. of Aristotle than the age of Franklin Delano Roosevelt is from that of Alexander Hamilton. Yet Aristotle, in his famous treatise on government, deals with problems which are acutely actual at this moment, and he has a passage describing the reasons why democracies degenerate into tyrannies which is a far more accurate description of the rise of Fascism than are most of the analyses of our contemporaries.

The architects of the Constitution had the intention of making a republican and federal government which would endure with stability, insure justice, promote the general welfare and be proof against usurpation, either by the few and the rich or by the poor and the many. For the founding of a republic they had guides. For a federal system they had none. But they thoroughly believed that help could be found in the successes and failures of the past. They knew all about the "class struggle"—so, for that matter, did the Greek philosophers, although you would think from our young socialist friends that Karl Marx was the first person ever to notice it. They knew all about Fascism and its causes, although they called it by another name. They knew the difference between a free state, a plutocratic oligarchy, a tyranny, monarchic or otherwise, and pure democracy. They set out to make a free federal state; and in doing so, they definitely rejected pure democracy, and for a very clearly seen reason: they knew that every attempt at pure democracy in the history of the world had quickly degenerated into tyranny.

It is important for us to be clear on this point, because words are used these days with extreme looseness. Since the last election, for instance, our form of government has repeatedly been said to be one of majority rule, and we are told that anything that the majority wants to do is justified under our system. Yet James Madison wrote in 1787 that one of the greatest dangers to popular government lies in the fact "that measures are often decided not according to the rules of justice and the rights of the minor party but by the superior force of an interested and overbearing majority." He said, "It must be concluded that a pure democracy . . . can admit of

53

no cure for the evils of faction . . . A common passion or interest will, in almost every case, be felt by a majority of the whole . . . And there is nothing to check the inducements to sacrifice the weaker party or an obnoxious individual. Hence it is that such democracies have ever been spectacles of turbulence and contention . . . and have, in general, been as short in their lives as they have been violent in their deaths."

It was precisely to guard against the dangers of usurpation, either by a willful man, or by an oligarchy, or by the majority—usually expressing themselves through some demagogic leader —that they planned a division of the powers of government. They knew that this would not promote the greatest possible efficiency; they knew that benevolent tyrannies—of which we have so many modern equivalents—are far more efficient and often enjoy immense popular favor. But they also knew that tyrannies, benevolent or otherwise, seldom survive the lives of their founders. And like all the great political historians and thinkers from Plato to the present day, they were convinced that from the viewpoint of man's dignity, development, progress and ultimate well-being, tyranny, however benevolent, is, of all forms of government, the very worst. And man's dignity, his spiritual role on earth, concerned them. And it was for the same reason, in their case fortified by their recent experience with George III, that these extraordinary men not only divided the powers of government but set definite limits to those powers, reserving whole spheres of life into which government might not penetrate at all. This, in fact, was one of their leading contributions to human freedom.

They were extremely realistic men, under no illusions about human solidarity. They knew that man is a creature of passions, self-interest, aggressiveness and credulity. Nevertheless, they believed that there *is* a political solvent. They did not believe, for instance, that all men are creatures of blind forces, economic or biological, and wholly determined by whether they are poor or rich or belong to this or that race. They believed passionately in man's capacity for reason, and in the duty of government to appeal to reason, as the essential arbiter for its actions.

If one compares the tone of public debate today—for instance, in the recent debate over the reform of the judiciary—with the tone of the debate over the acceptance of the Constitution, one is amazed at how the level has fallen. The issue at stake in 1787 was one of the greatest in human history. It was, essentially, whether the United States should become, like Europe, an agglomeration of independent states, eventually, perhaps, with separate tariff, military and diplomatic establishments, or whether it should be one nation. Actually, the country was suffering from "popular convulsions, from dissension among the states, and from the actual invasion of foreign arms." Yet, in presenting the national cause to the people, John Jay said:

"This plan is only *recommended*, not imposed, yet let it be remembered that it is neither recommended to *blind* approbation nor to *blind* reprobation; but to that sedate and candid consideration which the magnitude and importance of the subject demand."

Our Government, then, was founded on a belief in principle, embodied in law, and in the processes of human reason and deliberation; its architects repudiated the idea of unchecked majority rule, believing that protection for minorities is of the essence of free government; it attempted to keep a balance between factional interests; to provide checks against usurpations, whether by individuals, by oligarchies of the rich or by even majorities of the poor; and to leave in society itself a large area for voluntary action, whether by individuals or by groups of them.

From a purely governmental standpoint, this has been, for one hundred and fifty years, the American idea. Do these principles still have validity? Are they outworn and no longer workable? Have we departed from them; and if so, where and when? Do they imply conditions among the population which no longer exist?

There is no one "yes" or "no" to these questions.

V

THE idea that the powers of government should be limited did not originate with the framers of the American Constitution, although, in the Bill of Rights, it was more clearly embodied in a governmental document than ever, up to that time. But the men who designed our governmental structure were products of a revolutionary period of history—of the eighteenth century, which was distinguished by the rise of Liberalism.

The word "Liberal" has now become so variously interpreted that few people know what it means. Those who use it most precisely today are the Fascists and the Communists. They know what Liberalism is, and they are against it. For these people are collectivists. They believe in an economic order which is "total," in which the whole work of society is planned and directed by an overhead body, through the state. That body may be set up in several ways, either through a party directorate, as in Russia, or through a hierarchy of guilds, as it is, theoretically, in Italy; there are many different proposals as to how it might be constructed, many of them providing for a democratic base, but they all end in a similar picture. The individual is to become a *subject* of the state. However democratic the base, the apex of the pyramid is authoritarian, and the apex rules. For a planned society— or, as some people prefer to call it, a "scientific" society— presumes that the work and life of every individual will be planned, that it will be directed toward a defined goal—of so much production of such and such articles in such and such a time, under such and such conditions. As a matter of fact, no such plan, including the widely advertised Russian Five Year Plan, has ever really been made. Actually, "planned" nations have moved from improvisation to improvisation under the occurrence of unforeseen emergencies.

But, obviously, the concept that such planning is possible requires the presence of an unquestioned authority. For once the plan has been agreed upon—however democratically— it must be put into operation. It invariably begins by ordering production. But it must follow by seeing to it that consumers take what is produced. That involves collaboration from everybody.

Collaboration cannot be taken for granted, or even expected; there must be ways both of persuading it and of coercing it. Furthermore, a national plan cannot be changed from moment to moment by legislatures. Therefore, having once agreed on the main objectives—such as higher standards of living for the poor, general employment, the ending of the wastage of resources, national self-sufficiency, a balance between agriculture and industry, any large program which the people may consider desirable—the direct representatives of the people must delegate to commissions, or boards, or individual officials, the business of making the plan work.

These officials then become, inevitably, the government. For, entrusted with the task of organizing the whole production and consumption of a nation in harmony with a general plan, they set activities into motion which, if halted or radically redirected, will break down in general chaos, in which everybody will be involved.

The idea of establishing, first, a national objective, and then of organizing all individual activities in harmony with that objective, therefore *must* be accompanied by an eventual monopoly of all instruments which can influence opinion, by a tremendous enlargement of the police, by the suppression of all opposition, by the subjugation of science and invention, by the substitution of one political party for two or several, and by the eventual subservience of all the various instruments of government—legislatures, courts, local assemblies—to the real government, which is the body of officials charged to carry out the plan. It must, because otherwise the plan, which involves everyone's work, is constantly menaced. The real governors may be a dictator and his personal bodyguard, or an executive, or a planning board; legislative bodies may even continue to exist to rubber-stamp the activities of the officials.

The Planned Economy may call itself a Socialist Republic, or a Corporate State, or even a "Modern" Democracy. It may be set up in order to guarantee everyone an adequate income, or to establish universal equality, or to prepare the nation for greater glory; its avowed objective may be the national welfare, or the welfare of the proletariat, or the welfare of the race, or the welfare of the majority.

But whatever the objectives, once we accept the idea that the total labor of society shall fit in with a plan advanced by any authority, we begin to follow a pattern of organization which means the end of every kind of individual freedom. There is no such thing as partial economic dictatorship. Nowhere can you find an example.

This ought to be perfectly evident to anyone who opens his eyes and looks about him upon the world. The Communists and Fascists are engaged in a sham struggle of ideas. The actual forms of government under which Fascists and Communists live are almost identical. One claims to abolish private property and attacks the other as its defender. But the property of Russia is not controlled by the people, but by the bureaucracy, operating in the name of the people, just as it is in Germany, where you get your head cut off if you try to hold your property in gold or in anything except German paper.

What confuses the mind of the average American is that the American collectivist calls himself a Liberal, and has pre-empted a word which has a totally different philosophy behind it.

The Fascists and Communists know that Liberalism is their enemy. The Fascists, at least, are frank enough to say so. But the American collectivist, who calls himself a Liberal, believes that he can have the better of two worlds.

Yet everywhere, in the modern world, the way has been prepared for Fascism or Communism by people who championed the collectivist idea under the guise of Liberalism or Progressivism. Distressed by the obvious injustices and shortcomings of the society in which they lived, with the object of promoting the welfare of the masses, it was they who started setting up the all-powerful governmental machinery in which they were themselves eventually caught and ground to pieces.

In order to avoid a repetition in America of the recent history of part of Europe, it is urgently necessary for us to ask ourselves: What is a Liberal, and what are the fundamental principles of Liberalism?

VI

TO BE a liberal means to believe in human freedom. It means to believe in human beings. It means to champion that form of social and political order which releases the greatest amount of human energy; permits greatest liberty for individuals and groups, in planning and living their lives; cherishes freedom of speech, freedom of conscience and freedom of action, limited by only one thing: the protection of the freedom of others.

The American revolution of 1776 was a great liberal revolution. The Declaration of Independence and the American Constitution, more than any documents on earth, embody the fundamentals of liberalism. These documents assert the essential equality of human beings. This does not mean, and never did, that one man is as talented, or wise, or good as another, or that each person is entitled to the same rewards. It does mean that every human being has a right to his own life; that no man may be forced to labor against his will, or to assert beliefs contrary to his conscience, or be relegated to one class of society. It means that he has equality before the law: that all the rules of justice applicable to others are applicable to him; that he may not be arrested without a warrant, or tried without an indictment, or sentenced without a hearing. It means that a man shall not be prejudged or persecuted for causes which he cannot help. Since the passage of the Fifteenth Amendment, and the extension of universal suffrage, no person may suffer legal disabilities because of race or economic condition.

For the first century after the American revolution, the tendency in this country and throughout the world was to *liberate* human beings, and to equalize legal and social opportunities. Men were to be judged on their individual merit, not by the status of their fathers. At the same time, every attempt was made to enlarge the world for everybody, to increase the areas of the globe in which persons might move and work. Nationalism was an inclusive, not an exclusive doctrine.

The rise of liberalism was accompanied by immense technological progress; by the industrial

revolution; by the division of labor which en-
sued, and which suddenly, and prodigiously, ac-
celerated the efficiency of production; and by
the conception of economic life governed by the
market. In other words, of economic life governed by the buyer, not the seller. This was a
brand-new and wholly revolutionary idea.

Pre-eighteenth-century economics were governed, not by consumers, who determined what
should be produced by what they were willing
to buy in a competitive market, but by producers who enjoyed special privileges in return
for the most stringent kind of state regulations.
Mr. Walter Lippmann, in his book, *The Good
Society*, points out that in the days of Louis XIV
the manufacturers of France were told exactly
what to produce and exactly how to produce it.
Industry and agriculture were governed by
codes more complicated than anything ever invented by the NRA or Mr. Wallace. In the days
of feudalism all human relations were carefully
ordered and planned, and production was in the
hands of guilds, which controlled the market by
minutely ordering production. But the industrial revolution, coinciding with the rise of liberalism, brought forth the free market, the division of labor, the idea of production that would

be responsive to the demand, and the supremacy of the consumer.

The liberation of mankind from absolutist government and from rigid, authoritarian economic regulation had results not wholly advantageous. It destroyed a certain kind of security, and it upset stability. It changed a static, ordered world into a dynamic, and often chaotic, world. It increased in many respects the economic risks of existence. On the other hand, it distributed the strains, as they had never before been distributed.

And the gains were incredible. It increased and democratized the economic rewards as they had never been increased or distributed in the history of mankind. It gave impetus to invention and technique. It produced wealth at a rate which the world had never dreamed of. It made social classes elastic and impermanent. It stimulated the human imagination in unprecedented ways, by giving the mind room to breathe in. In a century it lifted the standard of living for the average man to a level which had previously been enjoyed only by the exceptionally situated, and in many ways above that level. It put on the breakfast table of the average man delicacies which kings, a century earlier, had not enjoyed.

The whole revolution was accompanied by a continually enlarging conception of human possibilities. For the first time in the whole of human history men could imagine a world in which no one need be ragged, hungry, cold. The mere conception of such a possibility was revolutionary. It was accompanied by a vastly increased sense of man's worth, by an increasing sensitiveness to the evils of poverty, pain and disease. Nothing, any longer, was taken for granted.

In previous epochs men, women and children had been laid low like frozen grass from obscure plagues, and these plagues had been accepted as acts of God. Now men investigated, questioned, experimented. They discovered that rats carried bubonic plague, that mosquitoes caused yellow fever; and lice, typhus; that women died in childbed from a doctor's dirty hands; they discovered the nature of bacteria, and the curative properties in the human blood stream. They traced diseases to forms of food. They developed inoculation.

Within a century they opened the utmost frontiers of the earth. Before the nineteenth century was over, they dreamed of conquering the highways of the air. The very elements of matter were being taken apart. The solidity of the earth, the elements of the soil were challenged. Matter was broken down into electrical energy, the soil into its chemical contents, and new sources of power were continually discovered.

The changing values of mankind began to be reflected in what they admired, in the very monuments they built. Men erected hospitals, scientific institutions, schools, bearing over their doors, not the names of kings, soldiers and potentates but of the new heroes of science, invention, technology and thought. Men began to dream of ending war forever.

Values changed. The ideal of the Middle Ages had been unity. The ideal of the eighteenth and nineteenth centuries was progress t h r o u g h infinite differentiation. The vast changes which were constantly taking place affected every phase of life, and often in a most upsetting way. The manner of living changed; the family changed; the nature of property changed. And these changes produced new social, economic and political problems, as well as new problems for the individual.

Industry concentrated workers in cities, and a new type of city came into being: the megalopolis, a gigantic monstrosity in which everything urban was present except urbanity, and every luxury available except neighborliness, quiet and fresh air. The same age that virtually stamped out smallpox saw men dying of tuberculosis in slums. The same age that put children into public schools put them into factories.

It is possible that man has moved too swiftly for himself. For these changes, adjustments and maladjustments have been so rapid that man has tended to lose sight of himself as a human being. In a remarkably short span of time, he has been stripped of traditional guides. The growth of the critical faculty has weakened his confidence in religion, as a guide to life and behavior. His very mobility, his unprecedented range of choice have put upon him responsibilities for decisions, often too hard to be borne. The dynamism of society is nerve-racking. Man no longer is sure even of himself. Science tells him that his body is a compound of electrical energy, that his emotions are the result of infantile and unconscious experiences, and that his behavior is dependent on the functioning of endocrine glands.

His horizons are beyond his vision. He finds himself equipped with extra hands and feet, and often with an external brain. He has ranging power over continents. He uses tools daily which he does not comprehend. He runs an automobile, but cannot describe its engine. He dials a radio, but cannot explain to his seven-year-old son what makes it go.

Everything in his experience has broken down the idea of acceptance and resignation. He has been taught to believe in the infinite perfectibility of everything. The emphasis on individualism and democracy has given him an exalted idea of himself and of the demands he is justified in making upon the world and society. The breakdown of religion has destroyed the sense of wonder. In a world of miracles he is without reverence.

The world is so obviously rich that he believes it richer than it is; nor has the average man the faintest conception of how so diverse and complicated a mechanism functions. If it fails to function smoothly, he demands that something be done. He calls in the government, with much the same certainty that he calls in a mechanic if the oil burner stops. He does not see that no more virtue or wisdom or intelligence resides in government than resides in the rest of society. He does not realize that government has only one thing not shared by other or-

ganizations and instruments of society. It alone
has force.

What we are seeing in the world today is an
enormous counter-revolution. In country after
country, under one slogan or another, the
people are retreating from freedom, and volun-
tarily relinquishing liberty to force and authority, with instructions to bring order into men's
affairs. They are affirming that the world which
their numerous energies have made has become
too complicated for them to run, and they are
delegating the power to run it to a dictator, or
a president, or the corporate state, or a political
party, or a planning board, or what not. But a
world subject to such fine, diverse and interdependent mechanisms cannot be run from the
top, except by enormously simplifying it.

The easiest way to simplify society is to reduce it to a military organization. That is the
most primitive form of social organization. And
that is precisely what is being done. The unit
of communal life shrinks. Wealth, prosperity,
inventiveness, choice, demand are subordinated
to simplified nationalistic aims. The very mind
which created the liberal universe becomes
atrophied through disuse. A dynamic society
becomes static. A new ruling class emerges—

of soldiers, bureaucrats and police. Such vitality as there is expresses itself in military adventures. The qualities which excite admiration, and have survival value, become the soldierly qualities—discipline, conformity, obedience, uniformity.

This, which is happening under our eyes, is a terrific and tragic spectacle.

For man, struggling under the responsibilities and disappointments of freedom, is retreating in very sight of the Promised Land. He is abandoning freedom at the moment when it can begin to be reconciled with an orderly world. And the whole world is preparing to go to war at the very moment when war is most utterly senseless, when it finds not only no moral justification, but is intellectually intolerable. Given fifty more years of the human mind operating freely, and mankind could be advanced to a grandeur and dignity which it has never yet enjoyed on this planet.

But that advance will take place only if free men will consider, with the utmost disinterestedness, wherein they have made their mistakes. Liberalism is not being killed by dictators. Liberalism is committing suicide—out of despair and a bad conscience. What liberalism needs is a revival, in the evangelical sense of the word. It needs to admit its sins, as the basis of renewing its life.

What have been its errors and shortcomings? When did it fall from grace? Can one retrace steps, and correct mistakes?

VII

ALL the political tendencies momentarily raging in our times are antiliberal. That is the outstanding fact about the era in which we live. The movement of the world is away from individualism, toward collectivism; away from freedom, toward order and organization; away from personal responsibility, toward discipline, obedience and acceptance.

This antiliberalism goes deeper than a mere desire to change a competitive economic order for a more co-operative one. In that desire there is nothing antiliberal. Antiliberalism seeks to subject the personality, with everything that the word means—conscience, responsibility, free will, the moral sense—to a pattern of work, conduct, behavior and belief imposed upon every member of society. The result of this tendency, carried to its logical conclusion, is the emergence of nations of slaves.

And, so insensitive has the liberal spirit become, that even people who call themselves liberals confine their main interest and argument to the question of whether or not the slaves are well kept!

And this happens after a liberal century—a century, to be sure, in which the ideals of liberalism have never been approximated, but in which the mere aura of them has added more to the wealth, knowledge and possibilities of human beings than has been achieved in any previous century in history. Why, then, is mankind revolting against liberalism, after so brief and incomplete an experience of it?

This question has concerned me more than any other during recent years. One can only try to answer it with humility. But the more I think of it, the more I am convinced that we have mixed up ideas and conceptions that have no real relation to one another. Above all, we have lost sight of the original purpose and philosophy of liberal democracy. We have come to associate liberalism with a certain kind of economics, and even with a certain stage of capitalistic development. To recapture and revitalize its original spirit would be, at once, revolutionary and conservative: revolutionary, because such revitalization would radically modify our present society; conservative, because it would link us again to our greatest traditions.

As I conceive it, liberalism is pre-eminently a type of mind, a kind of spirit and a sort of behavior, the basis of which is an enormous respect for personality. It is, therefore, above everything else human and humane. Its premise is that there is good in every nature; that a good society is the one in which that goodness can be given the greatest possibility to expand and develop; that this is the quality in man which sets him apart from other animals and therefore makes him human, and is the source of all social power, a constantly replenished spring of good will.

Liberalism—the doctrine of freedom—never, except thoughtlessly, conceived of itself as an end. It was only a means. Men and women must be free to experiment, to search, to question, to act—why? Obviously, that they may approach the truth. The object of liberty is to give men and women a chance to be their best selves. That is its first and last purpose.

If one goes back to the eighteenth century philosophers, who were the intellectual and spiritual source of the American revolution, one realizes that they are permeated through and through with the conception of man as an *ethical* animal. His business on earth is self-perfection. For self-perfection he needs freedom, because freedom and responsibility go hand in hand. It is not as an economic but as a moral being, in the first place, that man needs freedom. He needs it to realize his own spiritual possibilities. What those possibilities are is, fortunately, hardly debatable. You can read the poets and the prophets from Moses to the present day, and you will find that the same qualities of character and personality are admired.

In any civilization, and under any political system, the simplest mind recognizes a good person when he meets one. Courage, kindness, generosity and the sense of justice are his attributes. They are the perennial adornments of the human race. The very essence of liberalism is the realization that none of these qualities can develop to their fullest except in a fully responsible individual, who is free to act and to choose. A slave has no morality, because he cannot choose between good and evil. He has only a derivative morality—that of his masters.

One has to consider that from the time that men began to think, government was considered a Godlike attribute. Ancient kings, for that reason, traced their lineage from the gods, and governed by "divine right." Liberal democracy asserted the divinity in every man, and based his right to govern himself upon that divinity. Man was considered to be endowed with natural rights—the rights that were enumerated, for instance, in the Declaration of Independence —only because he was endowed with natural goodness.

Over and over again, in the writings of the founders of this republic, we come upon the idea that self-government implies the search for the public *good*, the consensus of the public virtue. William Penn summed up the ideal of human liberty in the remark: "Men must either be governed by God or they must be ruled by tyrants." Penn was a Quaker, believing in inner revelation through conscience, and for him it was self-evident that if men are to govern themselves they must be ruled by their own best natures.

It seems to me that liberalism has undone itself by forgetting these very simple and almost banal ideas which governed its origins. For the universal accusation against liberal democracy is that it has resulted in a society without standards. And yet no political philosophy ever started with so high a conception of the nature of man as liberal democracy. It did not think of him as primarily an economic animal—as a producer or consumer of goods, as a hirer or a hireling. It thought of him first and foremost as a human soul, capable of development and perfection. Certainly the hope of increased material well-being was part of the ideal—not a goal in itself.

Men were to be freed of poverty in order that they might become more human. Jefferson wanted to see the widespread distribution of private property, not in order that all men might enjoy luxury, but in order that they might enjoy independence, and therefore have courage and character. Walt Whitman, through whom flowed an almost mystical Americanism, repeatedly denounced the rising materialism of his times. He dreamed of cities invincible to the attacks of the whole of the rest of the earth, because they were cities of friends. He denied that the greatest city was the one with the tallest buildings and the longest bridges, but was that one which contained the largest number of great men and women. The creation of *people*, endowed with courage, independence, wisdom, was the American dream.

Liberalism, therefore, should have held constantly before its eyes the twin ideas of freedom and responsibility; self-expression and self-control; extreme tolerance of others, with extreme demands upon oneself.

The power and richness of this conception come from the very fact that it places so high a value on mankind, and, by placing the value, demands its justification. Everybody who has ever brought up a child knows how powerful a force in his development can be appeals to his pride, his trustworthiness, his desire to be thought well of, according to a high standard. The spoiled child is one who enjoys indulgences without reciprocal obligations. It seems to me that in a liberal democracy the overwhelming emphasis in all education should be upon encouraging the ideal of self-perfection and the most exquisite sense of obligation. Freedom, as surely as noblesse, obliges. But actually, the critics of liberalism accuse it of creating whole societies of spoiled children, societies clamorous with demands—demands from capitalists, from laborers, from farmers, and now from youth, who even go so far as to "demand" a creative life! The criticism has influence because it has truth!

There is an emotional power in the appeal to the best instincts of human beings which we sometimes see demonstrated in breath-taking ways. In times of great catastrophe—in fire, and in flood—we see quite ordinary people rise to heights of courage and generosity which are amazing. At such times there is an insistent demand from society upon the individual that he behave well—and, astonishingly, he does.

But by and large, in everyday life, liberalism has never even begun to draw upon the reserves of idealism and good will that are present in mankind. That has been its greatest failure. It moved away, almost immediately, from the original premise that man is a reasonable and moral animal, and that the object of society is to increase his reasonableness and his morality. Another conception perverted that idea, dominated most of the nineteenth century, and has gradually plunged the whole western world into moral chaos.

The idea of self-realization, of self-development—an athletic and robust idea, worthy of humanity—became perverted into the idea of self-interest. And for nearly three generations that perversion has dominated America. It is a mechanical conception that the unbridled competition of egoistic self-interests will work out automatically, in the long run, in the greatest good for the greatest number. A profoundly ethical conception gave way to a totally amoral one. The ideal of a society of individuals trying to *be* something, degenerated into the ideal of all individuals trying to *get* something. The love of fame—the ambition to be of good repute— degenerated into the love of money, of "success."

Self-interest has certainly not governed each of us wholly; for if it did, every personal relationship would disintegrate. But self-interest has raged through society, and bit by bit has disintegrated it, and the dictatorships are rising in the western world on the corpse of this idea of self-interest. It is played out; it is without validity.

Whole civilizations have fled into the arms of dictators, not only because the world has become technically complicated and difficult to run, but because human beings are lonely, fearful, without confidence in themselves or in one another, uncertain of why they were born and dissatisfied with their own behavior. People are actually welcoming enslavement, in order that, without liberty, they may at least have rest and the sense of being caught up into some purpose, however fantastic, however unrealistic, un-human and grotesque.

It is my belief that this tendency will be arrested by a new revolt in favor of liberalism. Not to believe it would be, for me, incompatible with faith in human reason and dignity. But the new liberalism must rise this time on the firm basis of its original humanism, as a form and mind becoming to man.

VIII

IF Liberalism has its roots in respect for personality, if it considers the means to be as important as the ends, and if its object is to release the greatest potential of human energy for good, what will be the attitude of the Liberal toward Government—and toward Capital and Labor?

The Liberal is not a follower of cut-and-dried formulas. Since his essential interest is in human freedom, and the development and expansion of the human personality, socially, and individually, and since this interest is founded upon faith in human beings, the Liberal is naturally cautious about all rigid restrictions. The Liberal regards the right to be let alone—to quote Mr. Justice Brandeis—as "the most comprehensive of human rights and the one most cherished by civilized men."

When the Liberal envisages an ideal society, he thinks of it as the one which is, to the greatest extent, self-regulatory. He would *like* a society governed by the golden rule, in which the individual thought of himself as a responsible and generous member of the group, and the whole group was sensitive to the needs and peculiarities of each of its members. But the Liberal is not Utopian. He is often less likely to be so than the extreme Conservative or the extreme Radical.

Radicals and Conservatives are not at all unlike, temperamentally. They want order, organization, efficiency, perfection. The Conservative or Reactionary thinks these can be best obtained by putting and keeping the power in the hands of a small class. He is afraid that an extension of democracy will destroy form and tradition, which he believes are essential to holding any society together. The Radical is so obsessed by the obvious faults of society that he wants to pull everything up by the roots and start all over again, and build a perfect society according to a blueprint. It is interesting that when the extreme Radicals triumph—in a revolution, for instance, as in Russia—they immediately become rigidly conservative, and punish all deviation rigorously. The worst fundamentalists in the world today are the Russian communists.

But the Liberal does not think of society as a mechanism, a hierarchy, an organization or a system. He thinks of it as a living organism, in which change is a matter of growth. He doesn't want to see it congealed in a pattern set by its ancestors, nor does he want to throw overboard all tradition and human experience. He is not prejudiced against anything merely because it is new, but neither is he prejudiced against something merely because it is old. He knows that at some time everything now old was new, and that it represented then, perhaps, progress. And if it has survived for a considerable time, he is sure that it must contain a strong element of truth. Therefore he tries always to make an integration, between what has been and what is becoming.

The essential mark of the Liberal is that he is against arbitrariness. He insists that every innovation justify itself in the light of reason. He is not at all impressed by size or numbers. He believes that an action, to be right, must be able to convince reasonable men, and not appeal for support either to the fact that "the best people" want it, or that a majority of the people desire it.

The Liberal believes in human nature, and

realistically affirms human nature. That is why he loves freedom. But he tries to appeal to the best in human nature, as represented by sense and reason. His ideal is to give people a break, a chance, and at the same time to demand from them a reciprocal spirit.

Instinctively, the Liberal tries to keep every phase of life elastic. He doesn't want today's reform to think of itself as the final good. Tomorrow will reveal something further, if only life is permitted to grow. He believes that, with sufficient leeway, mistakes will adjust themselves. They will be righted, if only the channels are kept open through which the mind and ingenuity of men can continue to flow.

This attitude of mind influences his day-to-day judgments about everything: about Capital, Labor and Government. Because he fears arbitrariness, he fears all concentrations of power, knowing that concentrated power means arbitrary control over human life. He is not, essentially, hostile to Capital, Labor or Government. But if any one of them becomes so powerful that it threatens to subject to itself the living organism of society, then he does his best to weight the balance against that threat.

A Liberal like Justice Brandeis believed thirty

years ago in this country that the enormous concentration of capital in huge corporations, each
of which controlled hundreds of millions of dollars and the work of tens of thousands of men,
represented a menacing concentration of power
without responsibility. Therefore he threw the
weight of his brilliant and eager mind and his
penetrating conception of law upon the side
of Government, as against Business, seeking
through law to check and mitigate this economic
power.

But a Liberal like Brandeis might very well
decide at another time and in another situation
that the menace of arbitrary power came from
another quarter than Capital. Thus on numerous occasions, while earnestly advocating trade-
unionism and fighting in the courts for the right
of Labor to organize and bargain collectively,
he warned that unions, also, could become a
menace, that the closed shop would eventually
lead to a labor monopoly, and that labor power
could be used against the general welfare as well
as for it. And similarly, when as a member of
the Supreme Court he voted against the NRA,
it was because he thought the National Recov-
ery Act delegated too great and arbitrary power
to a semi-governmental agency.

The Liberal is distinguished from the Conservative and the Radical, not only by his basic philosophy but by his methods. Never does he believe that a good end justifies an evil means. He seeks to find everything that binds men together, rather than what divides them, for he loves persuasion and detests coercion. He does not think that a decent and humane world will be made by appealing to the most aggressive instincts: by setting class against class, and section against section, and nation against nation. He believes that all men are held together in some degree by reason and common interest. And he is constantly searching for that common interest, as a basis of law.

He is impressed with the interdependency of life. With what Goethe called "its intimate integration." Therefore he looks before he leaps, and thinks before he acts. For he has great respect for this intimate integration and doesn't want to throw monkey wrenches into it.

Since his faith rests in the common sense of the human race, the Liberal is the great mediator. At this moment, in this country, it is his business to seek to bring together business, labor and government, and anyone who is trying to push them apart into hostile camps has no right to call himself a liberal. He will insist that business mend the vices which, in the past, have been the cause of rebellion and discontent, and he will co-operate with all attempts to find just laws to guard against a recurrence or continuation of excesses.

But as new laws extend fresh powers to other groups, the Liberal will insist that those powers also be attended by responsibility: that labor unions must conform to certain standards of behavior, that they keep contracts, publish accounts, establish no monopolies and abjure violence.

And the Liberal will also demand that if Government extends its operations into new fields, it do so under standards as rigorous for itself as it demands of others: that if it goes into enterprise, it establish a fair basis for competition; that it conform to principles of accountancy; and that it take complete responsibility for each of its acts—and not just for its general objectives and general program.

Some people say that liberalism is dead in the world—this sort of liberalism. But actually, I am sure, there are more liberals in America than any other kind of mental animal.

IX

MANY, many times I have thought that if there is to be a revival in the world, or in this country, of the truly liberal spirit, it will come through the influence of women. What is wrecking the world today is hatred and intolerance; simply that and nothing else. The problems of economic and political reorganization posed by man's own genius are, probably, insoluble, in any definite and final sense, since life is dynamic and eternally changing, and only a world of robots could be perfectly organized to function like a machine. But the object of mankind is not to live in a perfectly functioning universe, but to live in a tolerable universe, which means one suited to the nature and aspirations of human beings. We may eventually organize a world in which nobody ever is hungry, cold and unsheltered, and certainly it is possible to organize one in which nobody is ever unemployed. Dictatorships have demonstrated that.

But the object of being alive is not encompassed by these definitions. We want to live in a world in which we have such things as contentment, freedom, personal pride, opportunity for self-development, love, affection and spiritual purpose. We want to live in a warm world, a kind world, a human world. We want to be on good terms with ourselves, and with one another. And whatever new program or governmental system fails to assist these very simple human desires is a ghastly failure, even if it produces more goods, greater wealth, more economic stability and more national power than have ever been produced or concentrated before, and distributes them more equitably.

I think very often, these days, of my own childhood in an upstate New York Methodist parsonage. According to the standards of today, it was a childhood extremely limited, and even impoverished. I am sure, for instance, that the food that we had to eat was deficient in the properties which are recognized today as essential for a "minimum standard" of nourishment for relief cases. A green vegetable in winter was unknown, and an orange was a Christmas treat. We shuddered through the winters with continual drippy colds, sheltered in stove-heated houses, or houses warmed by hot-air furnaces that concentrated the warmth in the lower floors and left the bedrooms icy. And the preacher's children suffered many a school humiliation from having to wear unbecoming clothes, cut down from their elders', or handed down by a distant cousin.

Yet my own childhood was bathed in warmth and light, which was nothing but the irradiation of a beautiful personality, a man whose whole being was warmth and light: my father. His intimate belief in the goodness and justice of God, his unconquerable faith in the inherent decency of men, made him a creature radiating cheerfulness, even gaiety, turning every misfortune into a challenge or an only half-rueful joke; or, if it were a *real* misfortune, like the death of my mother, accepting it with a sweetness that was eternally impressive. And when he died, hundreds of people came to his funeral, not because he was "successful" and a celebrity —he never was—but because they loved him. His was the liberal spirit. Liberal, in the sense that we use the word when we speak of "liberal arts." Humane, rooted in humanity, caring for human beings, not as producers, or consumers, or workers, or employers—but as human souls.

From the viewpoint of such a personality, rooted in respect for himself, his neighbors and the world at large, the present world is intolerable. It is intolerable because of the rancor, hatred, contests for prestige, and class, race and international struggles, aggravated nowadays by actually being embodied in "philosophies." It is intolerable that men should be ruthlessly exterminated for differences of political opinion, as they are in Russia—as though "opinions" were the chief force binding mankind together. It is intolerable that a whole race should be indicted and banned—each individual, good, bad and indifferent, lumped into one category—as the Jews are in Germany. It is intolerable that we should accept the principle that there is a permanent, irreconcilable and even necessary hostility between workers and the men who employ them—as is positively implied in this country, in the National Labor Relations Act. For is it not clear that under *any* economic system there will be workers and directors, and if one destroys utterly the spirit of collaboration, how shall one revive it? It is intolerable, because these things are abuses of mankind by itself, a preposterous sort of self-flagellation and self-humiliation.

What every woman who is sensitive and conscious knows—and she may know it even if she isn't conscious, feeling it in her bones—is that in the America of today, as elsewhere in the world, there is a sterility in human relations, in the family, in the state, an atomization, loneliness, frustration, lack of warmth and juice, hatred, cleavage, shrillness, mechanicalness, heading toward new disciplines, which will not be self-imposed but coerced. And crying through the times is a gasp after the organic, the living, the vital, the human: richness, not in income but in the imponderables of life, such as serenity, faith, warm emotion, protectiveness, charity, affirmation—and even common sense! For what is common sense except sense and community, the individual and society, the person and humanity, not in contradiction, but in union, organically united, as the family is, or once was?

Someday, when women realize that the object of their emancipation is not to make them more like men, but more powerfully womanly, and therefore of greater use to men and themselves and society, this implicit demand and need of women for a world based, not on mechanical but on human principles, may break through as the most important influence upon history, and bring with it a renascence of liberalism and humanism.

X

MANY years ago the great English novelist, essayist and poet, George Meredith, made the remark that to believe that civilization is rooted in common sense is a first condition of sanity. This conception actually governed most thinking about society and politics throughout the eighteenth and nineteenth centuries, and almost until the present day.

In the eighteenth century they called common sense "Reason." Sometime, along about the time of the outbreak of the World War, the idea was abandoned by a great many people. There were good grounds for abandoning it, because it became apparent that however much lip service was tendered to Reason, it plainly was not the ruling passion of mankind. If it had been, there would not have been a World War at all. Woodrow Wilson's attempt to make a just peace, and to establish a genuine League of Nations, was perhaps the last grandiose tribute to

Reason that has been made in our times. And that failed too.

Since then every conceivable sort of Unreason has run amuck in the world. Here are just a few examples of totally unreasonable ideas that govern vast numbers of people:

First: the idea of national economic self-sufficiency. Science has struggled for years enormously to enhance the productivity of the globe. At the same time science has telescoped time and distance, and made the whole earth near neighbors, one of the other, with immensely improved systems of transportation and communication, while the diversification of labor has made everybody more interdependent than previously. And the whole Western world shares a common science, a common art and a common literature.

A discovery or invention in Berlin is quickly recognized and copied in Baltimore; a great play is to be seen almost simultaneously in New York, Paris and London; the pictures of famous artists travel from capital to capital; and works of literature find publishers immediately in a dozen languages.

All Reason, therefore, says that the time has come to abandon extreme nationalism, and to begin to conceive of the world as a single economic and cultural unit, or certainly so to recognize the Western world.

But instead, the twentieth century is marked by a resurgence of the most extreme nationalism, and with international markets glutted with cotton, tobacco, wool and every conceivable kind of food, whole populations, in numerous countries, live off rations limited to what they can grow at home; and in Germany the little children born in the last five or six years are growing up distinctly malnourished, suffering a self-imposed blockade as virulent as the one which the Allies atrociously inflicted upon Germany between the Armistice and the signing of the treaty.

Day after day, in pamphlets, books, newspapers, on the air and in the speeches of agitatorial leaders, ideas are promulgated which will not stand the light of Reason and Common Sense for an instant, and yet millions follow them.

As a second instance: A great world movement preaches that the whole of civilization rests on the shoulders of an exploited proletariat, and that the proletariat must take it over and run it. Actually, a moment's thought suffices to make one see that the tragedy of the industrial worker is not that he is exploited but that the common workman becomes less and less necessary as machines are invented as a substitute for the brawn and muscle that once could be exploited. The exploited proletariat of the twentieth century is a robot which asks only oil and gasoline or electric current for a diet.

Modern industry is such an incredibly complicated integration of immense capital investment, plus machinery, science, research and management, that the idea of turning it over to the proletariat, most of whom have not the foggiest notion of how any large-scale unit of the whole functions, is hair-raising to a reasonable man. In any highly industrialized country such a revolution would mean total breakdown, and starvation for millions—including, of course, the proletariat. Yet the idea appeals to many people, including a great many university graduates and students.

So does the idea of turning over this whole mechanism to the good graces of politicians, as personified in the State. The fathers of American Democracy had no exaggerated respect for the State, because they were pre-eminently men of reason and common sense. They never, for instance, identified the State with the People. They knew that the State is, by very definition, an instrument of oppression and coercion, and their idea was to make it strong enough to keep order and ward off enemies, and limit it otherwise very strictly. The idea of the State being a sort of apotheosis of the People, their ultimate expression and good, was invented for the modern age by the German philosopher, Hegel, and both Karl Marx, the father of Communism, and Mussolini, the inventor of Fascism, got their fundamental philosophy of politics from Hegel. But now this mysticism of the State, this distorted Hegelianism, which is a mysticism, and again cannot stand the light of either reason or common sense, infects the thinking of people all over the world.

The last two centuries and the intimate exchange of populations, ideas and cultures have also brought about an enormous mixture of all white racial stocks. Nowhere has this been carried on on a larger scale than in the United States of America. But in all European countries it has gone so far that there is not a single "pure" European race in existence. Even the Jews, the most exclusive people on earth, isolated for centuries both by their own desire and by force of circumstances, have become so racially mixed with the rest of the population that it is impossible to unscramble them, and among them are to be found every conceivable racial type, from pure "Nordic" to extreme Eastern European. And even Shakespeare told, in *The Merchant of Venice*, an enchanting story of the marriage of the lovely young Jewish Jessica to Lorenzo, a Venetian gentleman. Yet we actually see in our own day a recrudescence of "racialism," for which there is not an ounce of scientific justification, and millions follow this Unreason.

Not all the unreasonable fetishes of the modern age have originated in the dictatorships. Not by any means. There has been for years, in this country, a viewpoint held by a majority of both labor and businessmen that imports of foreign goods are a catastrophe. Quite the contrary can be proved. But under the Hoover Administration this belief was so widely held that we lent hundreds of millions of dollars abroad to prevent the political and economic collapse of Europe, while rigidly shutting European goods out of one of the world's richest markets. It was not until the whole policy blew up with a bang in a depression that cost more than the World War that a few people began to see a little light.

One could multiply indefinitely the Unreasons under which populations have lived; and it would, perhaps, lead many to the conclusion that the human race is hopelessly stupid, and that there is no hope for it. But a thousand triumphs of Reason could be cited. Man has a glorious history to prove how infinite are his faculties.

It would appear, however, that we have not even begun to apply the scientific spirit, the inquiring mind—Reason, and even its lesser brother, Common Sense—to our communal affairs. If we had, we would certainly not have the systems of taxation that we do. If we had, we would certainly not have the waste that we do. If we had, we would certainly not have nincompoops occupying positions of enormous responsibility and power in the field of politics. If we began to apply Reason we would abandon the idea that the net result of political bargains struck between pressure groups constitutes democratic government. And we would return —and in returning go forward—to many of the ideas set forth in the greatest American political document, The Federalist, and begin again to conceive of government as essentially deliberation, the object of which is to apply Reason to public problems, with the welfare of the whole in mind.

We would not try, either, to make Rome over in a day. We would concentrate on a very few extremely important things, and work experimentally, taking time to observe results.

XI

I HAVE long believed that we ought to introduce into our government practice something equivalent to the British royal commission. In Great Britain, when serious public problems seem baffling, and various pressure groups have various remedies, each based upon its own self-interest, it is the custom to appoint a royal commission, and charge it to prepare an analysis of the problem and recommendations for its solution.

The men who serve on these commissions are chosen for outstanding knowledge in the particular field under review. They are selected from a strictly nonpartisan viewpoint. Usually they contribute their services, for to serve on such a commission is a public honor.

They receive sufficient time and a sufficient appropriation to enable them to undertake careful research. Their findings are then published. The press of the whole nation comments on them. Often they will include a majority and a minority report. If all the members of the commission do not agree, particularly in proposing remedies, alternative programs may be submitted. And these reports then become both a means of educating the public to a disinterested and realistic view of the problem under consideration, and of influencing the legislation of Parliament.

The royal commission is, therefore, a fact-finding and advisory body to legislators, a body which continually introduces into legislation reason, realism and disinterestedness.

In our own country we have a series of "brain trusts" whose advice, however, is tendered not to the legislators, and not to the public, but secretly to the President. Their composition is almost anonymous. They do not come out with their advice, prepared to take responsibility for it, but express themselves like ventriloquists, through speeches which other people make, and bills which congressmen sponsor though they are not their authors. Neither the research nor the reasoning of these kitchen cabinets is a subject for public discussion. And, as a result, much of our legislation is ill-conceived and extremely dubious, and every mistake is costly.

We need, right now—we have needed for a long time—such a commission to present to Congress and to the American people a study of unemployment. For unemployment is the greatest single problem that confronts us. It is really our only serious problem. I think it is incontrovertible that the class struggles, violent lawlessness, revolutionary movements, racial and minority persecutions, autocratic bureaucracy and regimentation—all characteristic of these times, both here and abroad—arise from one primary cause: competition among human beings for an insufficient supply of jobs—that is to say, for an insufficient supply of the means of life!

In the past five years we have taken all sorts of measures to combat unemployment, but we have never, as the basis of Government programs, made a far-reaching and fundamental study of what the problem really is, from what it arises, how it divides into sub-problems, and what sort of private and public program is essential to deal with it in a thoroughgoing fashion.

One group says that it is "technological" and another vehemently combats that idea, insisting that technology creates far more jobs than it displaces.

But what, anyhow, is technological unemployment? Technology certainly continually changes the qualifications demanded from a worker. The man or woman who has nothing to offer except his hands, his brawn and muscle is today, to a large extent, unemployable. The agricultural worker who can do nothing but follow a mule or horse along a furrow finds his work without a market, for on the modern farm the worker needs to be something of a mechanic, something of a scientist, and have willing hands as well.

We have the phenomenon that, while there are millions of people out of work in the United States, there are thousands of jobs looking for men and women to fill them—and not finding them.

A real study of unemployment would probably reveal that our educational system is defective. That we are bringing up far too many "white collar" workers—and they, too, sloppily trained—and not nearly enough skilled artisans and mechanics.

Such a study should also consider population trends, particularly the population recession which is already setting in here in America. Eugenists have been calling our attention for years to the fact that the American population is receding; that the surplus of births over deaths is rapidly decreasing; that the average age of population is advancing. May it not be, therefore, that in foreseeable time we shall actually have a serious labor shortage? If this can be calculated, it would affect whatever legislative measures we may take.

And such a study would also reveal, unquestionably, that our population is being augmented in those parts of the Union that are most backward, culturally, economically and physically—the deep South, where inbreeding, poverty, illiteracy and disease are higher than elsewhere. Are we, therefore, adding to the unemployables of the next generation?

To what extent does the program of sharing the work, by radically shortening the working week, actually decrease unemployment? This question is vital, for most of the trade-unions of the country accept it as axiomatic, that the more you reduce the working week, the more jobs there will be for everybody. Yet the experience of other countries, particularly of France, would seem to indicate that this is a complete fallacy. If it is, the people of America, and above all the workers of America, ought to know it.

To what extent do trade-union policies, any-how, ameliorate or aggravate unemployment? We need disinterested opinion on this subject. The matter needs to be taken under review by men who are not the stooges of either the trade-unions or of business.

Periodic increases of unemployment are due to the ups and downs of the business cycle; and, incidentally, none of the collectivist nations have been able to abolish these ups and downs. They meet them by heavy armament programs or military adventures. Many people believe that the spending power of government could be used to keep employment steady, by launching large-scale public works, the moment unemployment passes a certain level. The expenditures from the public purse, thus made, would give a fillip to production and so reverse the trend. Then, when it is going again, under its own steam, the works as finished can be abandoned and the workers reabsorbed into private industry, until the next slump.

This formula seems reasonable, but we have not even started a long-range program for putting it into effect. To do so we would need, first of all, a means of keeping a continual month-to-month census of unemployment, in a more efficient manner than we now have. Then we would need a national planning board, as detached from politics as the War College is, to plan with the states exactly what should be undertaken as a crisis arises. Is it not weird that if Japan should attack us tomorrow, the departments of War and of the Navy would know exactly what strategy to follow? They have worked on it for years! But if unemployment attacks us tomorrow there is no instrument of Government that has a real program.

The WPA sprang into being in the last depression—or should I say the still-current one? —not as the result of any "plan," not after careful consideration, but because it popped into the heads of a few people. And we set up, almost overnight, a special kind of work society, separated from the ordinary working world, prodigiously costly, difficult, now, either to modify or to liquidate, and we have not even had any fundamental study made of its effects! We get a lot of propaganda from the WPA organization itself, and a lot of criticism from hostile political groups, but levelheaded analysis is what we need, not press-agent reports from one side or the other.

So long as we proceed in this manner, the

problems of our society will remain insoluble. For we do not even have a reasonable procedure by which to attempt their solution. We have merely the guesswork of an anonymous secretariat, mostly consisting of second-rate minds, congressional barter of votes for one bill in return for votes for another—largely determined by sectional interests, ballyhoo emanating from political parties and from press conferences—and all this in a world where representative government is being severely challenged. It will be more than challenged, unless it improves its techniques.

The women of this country could make over, if they wished to do so, the procedures of government. They could insist on having programs based upon thorough investigation by disinterested sources. They could insist on having basic problems removed from the field of class and sectional warfare and considered in something resembling a scientific spirit.

XII

THE pioneers of birth control are celebrating a long-fought-for victory: the legal recognition of the physician's authority to give information regarding contraception. For those who believe that it is a human right and duty to extend as far as possible conscious, intelligent control over mankind's destiny, the victory is a real one.

But the scientists have a word to say on another phase of this question. Mr. J. V. de Porte, of the New York State Department of Health, has said, "In New York State we are already in sight of the demographic equinox." Those are two-dollar words to describe the point when deaths and births exactly balance, and the population, thereafter, begins to decline. Not long ago Dr. Earnest Hooton, Harvard Professor of Anthropology, stated in a public address that humane measures to keep alive the unfit and prolong old age—while the birth rate declines—

were increasing the numbers of the inferior, giving us an old population and diminishing the level of general intelligence. An English scientist, Dr. A. M. Carr-Saunders, has published a study of world population in which he predicts a "catastrophic decline in the birth rate" in England, in the next fifty years. And both he and the Swedish professor, Gunnar-Myrdal, say that the same thing is happening all over the western world.

In Sweden a government commission has been appointed to investigate population decline and suggest remedies for halting it. They have found that in the enlightened city of Stockholm fewer than 5 per cent of families have three children or more, and less than 12 per cent have even two children. The Swedish people, their scientists warn, are dying out. And naturally they ask, why? Sweden is a highly civilized, free, democratic and relatively prosperous country. What will become of mankind's progress, if the race dies on the path? Is mankind losing a fundamental biological urge: the philo-progenitive instinct?

The Swedish commission finds that families living in large towns have smaller families than those living on the land. That is also true everywhere else. In America our population is augmented, not from the centers of industry but from the poor, backward but agricultural South. In Sweden the commission blames housing conditions for the passing of family life in cities. It points out that the average city family must pay from a fourth to a third of its income for rent, and that every extra room is at a premium. The average town dweller, unlike his ancestors, lives in one, two or three rooms and a kitchenette, where a child is a nuisance. That family has better living conditions today than its parents did, if one considers electric light, refrigeration, modern cooking, central heating and elevators, but it does *not* have room. And what is true of Stockholm is certainly true of New York and other big cities here at home. The young couple, living on a small salary or wage, may save enough money to have a baby or two, but it's the upkeep that counts, and that usually means a bigger apartment and more rent.

Plainly the answer to this is better housing, at cheaper prices, with government subsidy if necessary. In Vienna, during the Social Democratic regime, superb apartment houses were built with government aid in which the apartments were small, but were supplemented by splendid outdoor playgrounds in tree-shaded, enclosed courts, and by communal playrooms and kindergartens as part of the houses themselves, all under the same roof. Those who fight for better and cheaper housing today are not only fighting for the health of today's children but for the chance of tomorrow's children to be born at all.

But the Swedish commission not only blames housing and other economic conditions. It says quite bluntly that the love of comfort, even of luxury, is deciding the Swedish middle classes not to have children. They are a bother and they mean a sacrifice.

That, I am sure, is also true here; but to it I would add something else: an exaggerated idea of what parents *owe* their children.

What *do* parents owe their young? They owe them a decent inheritance of health, untainted by congenital disease, and society owes it to itself to demand greater eugenic control over prospective parents. Then, parents owe their children a home free from domestic strife and wrangling. They owe them an atmosphere of family consideration and affection. They owe them adequate food, but they do not owe them luxurious food, and if all the current ideas on diet are correct I do not see how most of us ever grew up. And they owe them an education to the point where they can shift for themselves. Above all, they owe them a pattern of behavior which the children may be proud to follow. Part of the material side of this debt society should, and does, help the parents to discharge, and it is possible that someday society may help even more.

But parents do *not* owe their children every luxury, the indulgence of every whim and fashion, complete lack of responsibility through childhood and youth into adulthood, moving pictures whenever they want them, motorcars —even secondhand ones—college educations, and security for life. The really superior high-school student who towers well above the average of his mates can get a college education today without the aid of his parents. Many of those whose harassed parents send them to universities at vast sacrifice would be better equipped for life by an apprenticeship or actual experience at a trade. The spoiled child is a peculiarly American phenomenon: selfish, demanding, pampered far beyond the necessities of his years, growing up to expect from society what he has always had from his parents—returns entirely incommensurate with his own contributions.

The men and women whose achievements adorn our society have seldom come from wealthy homes. They have also seldom come from deeply impoverished ones. They have had parents who accepted responsibility, set standards, had the courage to say "no" to their children, and early made them aware of the limitations of other people's generosity. They may not have had "advantages," but they had the tremendous advantage of cheerful, robustly sensible parents, with ambitions beyond a high-priced motorcar.

Therefore, neither their temporary comfort nor the apprehension that they cannot give their children vastly more than they ever had themselves is sufficient reason for many women not having children. Among my personal acquaintances I can count a dozen women who postponed having children in their youth for one of these two reasons. Almost all of them have lived to regret it bitterly. Their lives after thirty have been spent seeking advice as to how they can now have children, only to find that they have missed earlier opportunities and it is now too late. Looking ahead, a decade ago, they were afraid. Looking back now, they say, "we could have managed it, after all."

There is something basically wrong with a society in which the affirmation of life itself, the will to live and to create life, becomes atrophied. No amount of civilization, culture and technical achievement will save such a society in the end. The barbarians, with healthier instincts, will eventually inherit it.